great gardens
for kids

great gardens for kids

Clare Matthews

Photographs by Clive Nichols

Bounty
Books

First published in Great Britain in 2002 by Hamlyn
a division of Octopus Publishing Group Limited

This edition published in 2005 by Bounty Books,
a division of Octopus Publishing Group Limited
2–4 Heron Quays, London E14 4JP

A CIP record for this book is available from the
British Library.

ISBN 0 7537 1283 0
ISBN13 9780753712832

The author and publishers have made every effort to
ensure that all instructions and ideas given in this book
are accurate and safe, but they cannot accept liability for
any resulting injury, damage or loss to either person or
property whether direct or consequential and howsoever
arising. The author and publishers will be grateful for any
information that will assist them in keeping future
editions up to date.

Measurements Both imperial and metric measurements
have been given throughout this book. When following
instructions, you should choose to work in either metric
or imperial, and never mix the two.

Printed and bound in China

contents

introduction

With a little imagination and ingenuity, any garden, however small, can become a fascinating and stimulating place for children to play. More often, however, children's needs are poorly served in the garden – an afterthought resulting in some small concession or, more frequently, in a random assemblage of unattractive play equipment parents wish they could do without.

This book brings a creative, fresh approach to children's needs, and shows how to make unusual, captivating and attractive features which can be integrated into a family garden, or which can be carefully woven together to produce separate spaces dedicated to games, fun and fantasy.

Projects and inspirational case studies reveal practical and affordable ways any garden can be transformed into a children's paradise; a landscape that inspires imaginative play, provides physical challenges, appeals to the senses and nurtures an interest in nature and horticulture. In short, a safe place where children can explore, learn and relax on their own terms.

Clockwise from top left *Climbing Wall (see page 20), Wildlife Container Pond (see page 78), Rill (see page 50), Foldaway Playhouse (see page 28).*

The emphasis is on providing play features that children will really love – they are chosen with both children's needs and style in mind. Throughout the book, colour and decoration make a strong contribution to the projects and gardens, which are designed to appeal to children but are not childish. Whether the garden is traditional or contemporary, flamboyantly colourful or rustic, there are projects that can be tailored to suit each style and become a harmonious part of the overall design.

Creating a children's garden not only provides hours of happy fulfilling play, but addressing children's needs makes them feel valued and gives them a great pride in their garden. The more that children are allowed to contribute their ideas and take part in the physical business of a garden's creation, the greater that pride will be. All of the projects described here are straightforward and require no special skills, just enthusiasm and creativity on the part of both parents and children.

Above right and right *Plant a garden with all five senses in mind, to allow children to experiment with what they find around them. Touch is especially rewarding; choose plants with a variety of textures – smooth, soft, crinkly, rough, velvety or fleshy.*

Opposite page clockwise from top left *Pet Palace (see page 74), Strawberry Tower (see page 66), Daffodil Maze (see page 22), Sailing Boat Sandpit (see page 12).*

active play

Climbing, swinging, jumping, running and simply letting off steam are important parts of outdoor play. Using an imaginative approach, it is possible to create unusual and appealing equipment that provides the opportunity for children to test and develop their physical confidence while they play. A well thought-out array of equipment allows children to acquire skills and a confidence in their abilities, which can be learned in no other way. It is important that physical challenges are demanding, so the child experiences a real feeling of triumph and achievement. However, it is also important that steps are taken to make activities and equipment as safe as possible. However robust, equipment will suffer from wear and tear and should be checked regularly for signs of damage and fatigue. When planning an area for physical games, consider both the age and size of the children who will use it – if possible add elements which can be changed to provide new challenges, such as the Climbing Wall (see page 20). All the projects in this chapter are designed to look appealing and provide hours of really exciting physical play.

Sailing Boat Sandpit • Rope Spider's Web • Pebble Mosaic Hopscotch • Climbing Wall • Daffodil Maze

sailing boat sandpit

It is with good reason that a sandpit is considered an essential part of gardens for young children. Even the most modest sandpit can provide hours of amusement. Sand provides the opportunity for creative and constructive play, and is ideal for fine-tuning the motor skills of young children. What is more, it is a valuable prop in fantasy games, where even humble sand pies can become cream buns. Just provide assorted scoops, spoons, cups and buckets. Decorated as a sailing boat, this stylish sandpit has an added appeal to inspire imaginative play.

materials
large tyre
mid blue multisurface
   spray paint
bath sponge
bright blue acrylic paint
13mm ($^1/_2$in) diameter
   wooden dowel
tack
turquoise and blue kite fabric
weed-suppressing membrane
play sand

Choosing materials

Choose a clean tyre without any obvious damage. The kite fabric can be any colour you like; the beauty of it is that it doesn't need to be hemmed – simply cut it to size.

1 Thoroughly clean the largest tyre available and allow to dry. Paint it using a multisurface spray paint. Cut a bath sponge into a wave shape and, using acrylic paint, sponge waves around the tyre in a contrasting blue.

2 Make a hole for the mast in the wall of the tyre, using a 13mm ($\frac{1}{2}$in) wood drill bit. Push in the length of dowel and secure it in an upright position with a tack through the base of the tyre into the bottom of the dowel.

3 Cut a triangular sail from kite fabric to fit the mast, allowing extra width for a turning along its vertical side wide enough for the dowel to slip through. Sew the turning over and slip the sail over the mast. Top it with a blue flag made in the same way.

4 Line the base of the sandpit with weed-suppressing membrane or thick polythene sheeting and fill it with sand. It may be necessary to cover the sandpit when not in use to prevent animals from soiling the sand.

rope spider's web

This robust rope climbing challenge is enormous fun. Made from seemingly natural materials, this vast web is cunningly composed of a combination of simple knots, making its construction within the reach of anyone who can tie a knot in the corner of their hankie! Not only is the web superb for climbing and swinging, its unusual form makes it a splendid prop for fantasy games. The web can be adapted to fit any space, and also presents an attractive solution to separating or screening off parts of the garden. Though the rope used here appears natural, it is a craftily disguised synthetic rope. It is important to use a strong synthetic rope, as it will resist rot far more efficiently than natural fibres, which may perish in just a few seasons. As with all play equipment, however, it is important to check regularly for signs of deterioration.

materials
2 large wooden posts,
  4m (12ft) long
ready-mix concrete
30m (100ft) of 3-strand
  hempex rope
sticky tape

1 Dig two holes 1m (3ft) deep and 2m (6ft) apart, stand the posts in the holes and pack ready-mix concrete around them. Ensure that they are vertical. When the concrete has set, drill two holes 10cm (4in) apart near the top of each post and another pair about 30cm (12in) from the ground. Add another single hole at the centre point on both posts, making sure all the holes are at corresponding heights on the two posts.

2 Thread a length of rope through the lower of the top pair of holes on the first post. Pass it diagonally to the higher of the bottom holes on the second post. Take it back through the lowest hole on the same post to the lowest hole on the first post. Then back through the adjacent hole on that post and diagonally to the lower hole at the top of the second post. Pull the rope tight and secure it with overhand knots (see page 16).

3 Tie a length of rope between the two uppermost holes and another between the central holes. Again use an overhand knot to secure them on each side. Keep all ropes as taut as possible. Add a length of rope vertically across the centre of the web.

4 Attach it to the centre point of the uppermost horizontal rope using a cargo knot (see page 16), finished off with an overhand knot. Pass it across the centre, tying an overhand knot around the criss-crossing ropes and finish off with a cargo knot followed by an overhand knot at the centre of the lowest horizontal rope.

5 Starting from the centre, spiral the remaining rope round the framework. Start with a cargo knot finished with an overhand knot at the centre and tie a cargo knot each time the rope crosses another. Take care to keep the ropes taut, but do not distort the web. Finish off using a cargo knot followed by an overhand knot and the web is complete.

How to tie an overhand knot

An overhand knot is the simplest of knots. Simply loop one end behind the other, pass it through and pull tight.

How to tie a cargo knot

1 Cargo knots require passing one rope end through another. This process is made easier by binding the rope end with tape.

2 Start by passing the bound end of the rope up between the strands where you want the knot to be.

3 Take the end back round in front of itself, up behind the horizontal arm, back through the loop to the front.

4 Pull the rope taut and continue with the loose end. Use this knot to join one rope to another as you pass it.

Right *Here a crossbeam and ladder have been added to the sturdy structure for extra climbing fun.*

pebble mosaic hopscotch

Going from here to there is much more fun if it is done with a hop and a jump. This traditional game has been reproduced in attractive pebble mosaic paving stones. They can be set into a gravel or grassy path, arranged in a patio, or form stepping stones across a well-trodden patch of lawn. The mosaics are incredibly durable and deceptively straightforward to make. The same technique could be used to produce purely decorative stones with patterns, or perhaps initials or words.

materials
4 offcuts of timber, 2.5cm (1in)
    square and 30cm (12in) long
nails
black pebbles
white pebbles
polythene sheet
cement

1 Make a simple mould by nailing the four pieces of wood together into a basic square shape. Make the square the size you want the finished mosaic paving slabs to be.

Slabs with numbers can be laid out to form a hopscotch board. However, many different designs can be used – try initials, letters or simple patterns.

2 Using black and white pebbles, lay out the first number in the frame. Start with the border and the number in dark pebbles, then fill in the background in white pebbles. Any simple design will work. Carefully remove the frame to leave the pebbles in place.

3 Place the frame on a polythene sheet and almost fill it with cement. Transfer the pebbles from the design to the cement, pushing them well in. Leave overnight before removing the frame. The cement takes one week to reach full strength.

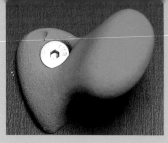

climbing wall

Perhaps the ultimate climbing challenge you can provide, this colourful climbing wall is straightforward to construct. It is made from two sheets of plyboard which are attached to vertical posts in the ground, and have climbing holds fixed to them. The aim is to progress along the wall without touching the ground, rather than climbing to alarming heights. Climbing only a small distance from the ground, however, does not diminish the task nor the sense of achievement as the child stretches arms and legs, clinging with fingers and toes to the holds. The climbing challenge can easily be changed and made more demanding by simply rearranging the holds. This wall is designed for pre-school children, but could easily be scaled up to suit older children.

materials

2 sheets of 18mm (³/₄in) marine
   plyboard
PVA primer
wood-preserving stain
climbing holds with T-nuts
5cm (2in) countersunk bolts
3 wooden posts, 7.5cm (3in)
   square and 2m (6ft) long
9 large bolts
ready-mix concrete

1 Coat the sheets of plyboard with a solution of one part PVA to one part water. Mark the positions of the holds and drill holes using a 10mm (³/₈in) wood drill bit at each location. Drill more holes than you have holds, so that the challenge can be changed later on. The distance between the holds should be challenging but not disconcerting.

2 Paint the boards with wood-preserving stain. Choose a colour to suit its location. This climbing wall is bright and cheerful, but choosing greens or browns would render it less obtrusive in the garden.

3 Securely push a T-nut into each hole in the board from the back. Attach the climbing holds to the front of the boards using the countersunk bolts to fix them in place. Take the time to devise a demanding climbing route across the wall, but also an appealing arrangement of holds in different shapes and different colours.

4 Bolt the boards on to the fronts of the three square posts, so that they form a continuous board. Use three bolts for each post. Dig three holes, 75cm (30in) deep, set the posts in position and pack ready-mix concrete around them in the holes. Ensure that the wall is held vertical until the concrete sets hard. The 'rock face' is now ready for climbers.

daffodil maze

More correctly, this sparkling display of the fragrant narcissus 'Yellow Cheerfulness' is a labyrinth of blooms. Two interlocked spirals of flower form a path from one side of the maze to the other, firstly spiralling into the centre and then spiralling out again in the opposite direction. This vast display is not only fascinating and attractive, it makes a wonderful place to play. Walking slowly through the maze, concentrating on every step is totally absorbing, but add some friends and the maze lends an extra challenge to lively chasing games. You can never be quite sure if your pursuer is on the same path as you. From the moment that the first shoots emerge, delineating the pattern of paths, the maze is a magnet to children. The flowers last six weeks in good conditions. Work starts on the maze in the autumn.

materials
2 long ropes
daffodil bulbs (about 150 per
    metre/yard of maze)
grit (optional)

1 Using two ropes, lay out the design. Ropes can be easily adjusted to get the perfect shape. If possible, check the design from above.

2 Laying out the bulbs around the maze will ensure you have sufficient for the proposed design. This maze has a diameter of 8m (24ft).

3 Arrange the bulbs in a single layer on the grass, closely following the lines of the ropes. Reduce the width of the lines of bulbs as they come towards the centre of the maze.

4 Lift out sections of turf to create planting areas about twice the depth of the bulbs. Arrange the bulbs randomly in the hole and replace the turf. Continue around the maze. If the soil is heavy and moisture retentive, add a layer of grit to the base of the hole before putting in the bulbs.

Using a bulb planter

For smaller designs, a long-handled bulb planter could be used. Simply remove a plug of turf with the planter, pop the bulb into the hole, pointed end upwards, then replace the turf and tread down lightly.

Below *As the bulbs emerge, the maze soon takes shape. As soon as the growth is obvious enough not to be trampled, play can begin in the maze.*

Left and right *The sheer exuberance of the* Narcissus *'Yellow Cheerfulness' makes it an excellent choice, plus it is a robust late flowerer which naturalizes well. This maze does require a lavish use of bulbs but they should return year after year, making the maze a seasonal treat, a celebration of the return of warmer weather. For a smaller space, the whole concept could be simplified – even a wiggling pathway of bright flowers and foliage could provide hours of entertainment.*

Left *After flowering, the maze must be left for six weeks before mowing, to allow the bulbs to build up energy for next year's flush of flowers, so a hidden corner may be the best location for the maze.*

a place
of their own

Whatever form it takes, children of all ages revel in the privacy and opportunity a place of their own affords. A playhouse, den or hideaway is an important part of any children's garden. For younger children, it is a secure intimate space where they can feel comfortable to initiate all kinds of fantasy play. Whatever the playhouse's actual shape, size or theme, in the powerfully imaginative mind of a young child it can become anything from a spaceship to a zoo, a stage for role-playing games. As children grow older, a den forms an important function as a private place to share with friends. A place to read, invent games and relax on their own terms.

In providing a playhouse or hideaway, there are a number of points to consider. First, its location; if chosen carefully, even a children's den can make a positive contribution to the appearance of the garden. Select a hideaway which is in sympathy with the style of the garden and plan its position carefully. What might look at home in a rural situation is unlikely to look appealing in an urban courtyard. Second, consider the ages of the children who are going to use it – a toddler paradise is unlikely to appeal to a seven-year-old.

Foldaway Playhouse • Flowery Hideaway • Suspended Tent • Vine Tepee

foldaway playhouse

Where space is limited, a playhouse which can be folded away is a splendid solution. Anchored to any solid vertical structure, this cheerful little hideaway takes only seconds to fold or unfold, bringing variety to the garden. The absence of a roof is irrelevant to younger children who will feel at ease in the intimate space the playhouse creates. There is plenty of room for two or three toddlers and their toys. Changing the painted decoration will change the appeal of the house. Painted brown it becomes a log cabin, paint it grey and add crenellations and it becomes a castle – the possibilities are endless. The playhouse is reasonably durable, but may need protecting from the worst of the winter weather.

materials

4 pieces of 8mm ($^1/_4$in) exterior-grade plyboard, 50x110cm (20x44in)

1 piece of 8mm ($^1/_4$in) exterior-grade plyboard, 120x110cm (48x44in) and rising to a point

PVA primer

acrylic paints

5cm (2in) wide Velcro fastenings

strong glue

staple gun

8 small blocks of timber

tacks

5 metal hooks and eyes

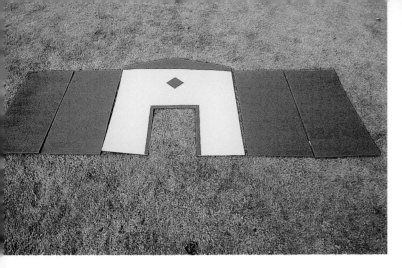

1 Cut the pieces of plyboard to size and seal the panels with a solution of one part PVA and one part water and leave to dry. Paint them with acrylic paint and leave to dry again. Lay the pieces flat on the ground face down, as if the house has been opened out.

2 Use strong glue and a staple gun to attach two sets of Velcro squares on one side of each panel so that it can be joined to the next. Fix the longer strips of Velcro to the opposite sides so the panels can be joined together to form the house.

3 Prop the house into position and tack a block of wood to each of the inside front corners at the top. Fix a metal eye on one block and the corresponding hook on the adjacent block on both corners of the house. Tack two more blocks on to the edges of the house where it meets the wall, and the remaining blocks on to the wall itself. Screw the eyes into the blocks on the house and the hooks on the wall to hold the structure rigid and secure.

4 To fold the house away, loosen the Velcro straps and unfasten the front safety hooks. Push the centres of the two sides towards each other to collapse the house. Use another hook on the reverse of the front panel to secure it to the wall.

flowery hideaway

The tiniest of hideaways are attractive to children. This flowering bower takes up little space and is appealing enough to take pride of place on the patio or even balcony; although it would look equally at ease set in an herbaceous border. The unexpected presence of a secluded space amid the flowers makes this secret hideaway especially appealing. The twining stems of clematis rapidly cover the framework; within just a few weeks there is a feeling of privacy. Carefully choosing the clematis ensures the bower is decked with colourful flowers throughout the summer, while a fragrant skirt of petunias clothes the sides of the pots.

materials
5 large pots
blue masonry paint
aluminium foil
newspaper
crocks
compost
5 clematis plants
petunia plants
5 iron poles
silver metal paint
galvanized wire

1 Choose five large containers. Here, inexpensive terracotta has been livened up with soft blue masonry paint. When the paint has dried, line the pots with aluminium foil.

2 Next line the pots with a good layer of newspaper, to help retain moisture and keep roots cool. Add a layer of crocks to the bases of the containers.

3 Fill with compost and plant the clematis 5cm (2in) deeper than in their original pots. This gives the plants a chance to regrow, should clematis wilt strike.

4 Next plant petunias around the edges of the pots. Place the five pots in a circle and, using five iron poles painted silver, create the frame of the tepee. Finish with a spiral of silver wire wound around the frame, leaving an opening to form the door.

Choosing plants

Choose a selection of plants to fit in with the colour scheme in your garden. These are **Clematis** *'Comtesse de Bouchaud' and 'Multi Blue', with* **Petunia** *'Pastel'.*

suspended tent

When suspended from any convenient tree or shrub, this brightly coloured tent makes a spacious den. The tent is crafted from kite fabric, which is durable, light and easy to work with, as it does not fray when cut. Simple sand bags weight the corners as a safer alternative to tent pegs, which could of course be used instead. Bright and cheerful, the tent provides an ideal temporary summer residence. Packed into a small bag, it is fun to take on holiday or even picnics.

materials
blue kite fabric
purple kite fabric
cotton
metal eyelets and
 fixing tool
sand
cleats

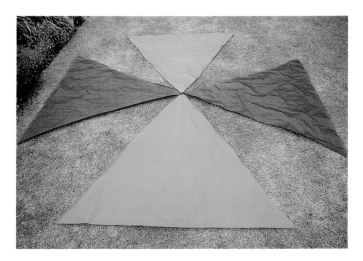

1 Cut four identical triangles of kite fabric, each with a base of 160cm (64in) and a height of 170cm (68in). Sew them together using simple running stitch, so that the colours alternate.

2 Fit a metal eyelet into each corner of the tent and another one through its apex. These simple eyelets are attached using a hammer and a special fixing tool.

The fixings

3 Use more kite fabric to create four sand bags, approximately 20x30cm (8x12in). Turn them right sides out, fill with sand, sew up the open edge and add a metal eyelet. Attach the bags to the corners of the tent using cleats.

4 Cut a 50cm (20in) vertical slit in the centre of one of the sides of the tent to create a door. Attach a cleat to the metal eye at the apex of the tent and use it to suspend the tent from a sturdy tree or shrub.

Galvanized cleats and eyelets are easy to find in hardware or sailing shops. The eyelets come with a special fixing tool which is simple to use. Make sure the cleats fit through the eyelets.

vine tepee

Swathed in a rustling cloak of enormous, beautifully textured leaves, this simplest of structures provides a snug hideaway. It fits well in a green or wooded garden, or it could even be tucked discreetly in among established shrubs. In the autumn, the tepee becomes a glowing display of some of the season's most spectacular colours. Here a vitis, a vigorous tendril climber suited to partial shade, has been chosen but you could experiment with other leafy climbers to suit the proposed location.

materials
about 18 sturdy hazel poles,
   3m (10ft) long
hemp twine
5 *Vitis cognetiae* plants

1 The tepee is formed with stout hazel poles; the floor area is about 2m (6ft) in diameter. Start by pushing five of the poles firmly into the ground to make a circle, allowing them to cross at the centre of the circular area. Tie the tops with twine to secure.

2 Add more hazel poles equally spaced around the tepee, not forgetting to leave a gap in the front of the circle to form the door. Tie all the rods securely together at the apex of the tepee using thick hemp twine, or other twine of a natural colour.

3 Cut three shorter lengths of hazel pole and tie them across the door space to leave just a small entrance at the bottom. Arrange five vines around the tepee, spacing them evenly.

4 Plant the vines close to the poles, angled towards the structure. Five plants give good coverage quickly, but fewer would do the job given time. Carefully encourage the vines on to the structure and keep well watered.

furniture

A table and chairs play a fundamental role in children's gardens, just as they do in one designed for adults. They are a focus for activities: they provide a place to eat, draw, paint, play and entertain friends. When choosing or creating garden furniture for children, it is important to consider the size of the children who will use it. Adult furniture is inappropriate for small children who have to make perilous climbs on to chairs and, once there, sit uncomfortably as they stretch to reach up to the table. Similarly, outgrown furniture would be uncomfortable for older children. Robust durability and safety are fundamental qualities to seek in children's garden furniture. Not only will it need to withstand the battering of the elements, it will also need to stand up to all kinds of rough treatment. Remember to make provision not just for your own children, but also your children's guests.

A place to eat or sit is best positioned slightly away from equipment designed for active play; the juxtaposition of two very different types of activities could easily cause conflict or even present a safety hazard. As always, ensure that the furniture chosen complements its surroundings. Decorative furniture can bring a vibrant splash of colour to the garden, while natural materials are less obtrusive. When thoughtfully placed, appealing furniture can also fulfil an additional ornamental role, providing an attractive focal point and drawing children into that area of the garden. The projects in this chapter produce simple, appealing furniture which children will really enjoy using.

'My Place' Mosaic Table • Grass Stools • Growing Bench

'my place' mosaic table

A table and chairs are a fundamental part of any children's garden. Here, a garden table past its best is given a new lease of life using richly coloured opaque glass mosaics and florist's beads. A randomly patterned background provides a foil for circular 'place mats' designed and completed by the children themselves, allowing each child their own individual creative input on a manageable scale as part of a larger family project. Mosaic is a wonderfully durable surface, with a timeless appeal. Any sturdy table could be used, so long as its size is appropriate to the children who will use it. Larger pieces of furniture could even be cut down if the integrity of their structure is preserved. If a wooden table is used, a coat of matching wood stain completes the transformation.

materials

2.5cm (1in) exterior-grade
  plyboard
PVA primer
screws
exterior tile adhesive
mosaic tiles
glass florist's beads
exterior tile grout

1 Cut the piece of plyboard to the exact size of the table top. Seal it with a solution of one part PVA to one part water. Allow to dry and screw it to the top of the table. Mark on the positions of the 'place mats' by drawing around a dinner plate. Mark guidelines along the centre of the board in both directions to give a centre point.

2 Apply the border tiles and those delineating the place mats by 'buttering' the back of each tile with tile adhesive and pushing it firmly into place, leaving a uniform gap between tiles.

3 Starting from the centre line and working out, randomly apply the background tiles. Cover large areas quickly by cutting the paper backing sheets of the mosaic tiles into blocks and pushing them evenly into a bed of tile adhesive applied to the table. Make the pattern random by cutting a few holes in the sheets and infilling with tiles of a different colour.

4 It will be necessary to clip tiles to fit around the 'place mats'. Use tile nippers. Score a line on the tile and break it using the nippers. (Wear gloves and safety goggles; this is not a task for children.) Leave to dry for at least four hours before removing the paper backing from the tiles, by dampening it and peeling it away.

5 Allow each child to work out the design for their 'place mat' on a piece of paper. Transfer the design into place on the table using either the 'buttering' method or pushing the pieces into a bed of adhesive.

6 When it is dry, spread grouting over the surface of the table, working it into the gaps between the tiles. Wipe off any excess with a damp cloth. Once dry, remove any final traces of grout on the tiles using a scourer.

grass stools

Placed around the garden, these grassy pots make wonderfully novel, child-sized stools. Here the pots have been painted a sunny yellow, but choose a colour to suit their location or let each child design and decorate their own stool. Camomile or creeping thyme would make interesting alternatives to turf, with the added appeal of a burst of fragrance each time they are used. Both plants would enjoy a sunny spot and can be trimmed to keep them neat and encourage a dense coverage. The stools, when weighted properly, are very stable but they are not suitable for young children to climb on.

materials
squat terracotta pots
masonry or acrylic paint
turfs
bricks
compost

1 Paint the pots using masonry or acrylic paints and allow to dry. Choose a colour to fit in with the rest of the garden.

2 When the paint is dry, invert the painted pot on a turf and cut around it with a sharp knife to cut out a circular piece of turf.

3 Pack the bottom of the pot with bricks to give it stability. Four bricks for each pot should be sufficiently heavy.

4 Fill the pots with compost to about 5cm (2in) from the tops of the pots. Firm down the compost well and smooth the surface.

5 Place the turf circle on top of the compost and gently firm it down. Water it well. A slightly domed finish is more attractive than a flat one. Keep the turf well watered and trimmed.

grass stools 41

growing bench

This sturdy bench is formed from thick slabs of natural wood. The towering back forms a trellis, which can support climbing plants to form a living screen. Set the bench 60–90cm (24–36in) away from a fence or hedge and it forms a leafy 'rat run' behind it, ideal for chasing games or hide and seek. It can also be used to divide one area of the garden from another. Many climbing plants will clothe the trellis. For the best effect, pick a plant which will thrive in your chosen location. Clematis will make a pretty, flowery screen, while humulus will produce a covering of lush lime-green leaves each year. For a more shady location, x fatshedera, as used here, will give a tropical feel to the garden.

materials
large slab of wood
2 logs
2m (6ft) garden canes
hemp twine
climbing plants, such as
  x *Fatshedera lizei*

1 Choose a large slab of wood to make the seat of the bench. Use two equal sized logs to support it. It is important to make the bench the correct height for the children who are going to use it.

2 Use a 13mm (^{1}/$_2$in) wood drill bit to drill a series of holes along the back of the seat. Space the holes 10cm (4in) apart.

3 Set the two log supports into position. Place the seat on the supports, ensuring it is level. Push a cane through each hole in the back of the seat of the bench and push it firmly into the ground beneath. This gives the bench stability. For even greater rigidity, the seat can be screwed to the top of the logs.

4 Tie three canes horizontally across the vertical canes, using hemp twine to secure. Ensure that there are no dangerous ends protruding which could cause injury. Prepare the soil behind the bench and plant your chosen climbers. Encourage their progress up the canes and keep well watered until they are established.

water

Children have a boundless fascination with water. Exuberant, splashing water play has an obvious appeal on hot summer days, but more measured experimental games are no less enjoyable. During this play, which allows the exploration, however unconsciously, of the properties of water, children learn about sinking and floating, volumes and displacement and the movement of waves and ripples. A creative provision for this type of fun adds greatly to the entertainment value of a children's garden. Ornamental features which have no expanse of open water are safer for areas where children play. However, they are seldom designed with play in mind. Children may enjoy the sensual pleasures of the sound of water and holding their hands in the water's flow, but they have no real play value.

The projects outlined here are specifically designed with play in mind. However, in providing any opportunity for playing with water, safety considerations should be paramount. Carefully consider the ages and capabilities of the children who play in the garden and always provide adequate supervision (see page 156).

Water Serpent • Seaside Wall Fountain • Rill • Bubbling Spring

Left *Yellow and green banners add height and movement to the garden. These are made from pieces of sheeting stitched together, with a sleeve stitched down the long edge. They are simply threaded on to garden canes. Inexpensive baskets with yellow and green bows are ideal for egg collecting. Each child can decorate their own before the hunt.*

How to dye eggs

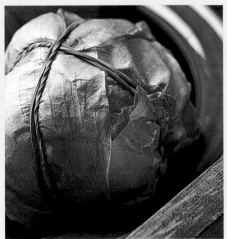

1 Traditionally, in many parts of Europe, eggs are dyed using flowers and leaves. Collect flowers and foliage from the garden.

2 Arrange the flowers and leaves around the raw egg and wrap in onion skins. Secure with elastic bands and hard-boil the eggs.

3 When cool, remove the wrapping to reveal the surprising patterns beneath. These eggs are for decorative purposes only.

Above *After an afternoon of hunting eggs and chasing around the garden, an alfresco Easter tea is much appreciated.*

Right *Shaped cutters and a little yellow icing make these basic homemade biscuits especially appealing.*

Above *Cheery purple violas make a perfect centrepiece for the tea table. Chicks on sticks add a touch of Easter fun.*

Right *A splash of green acrylic paint transforms a flower pot into a container for an abundance of chocolate eggs.*

Top *Give any small cake extra appeal with a topping of foil-wrapped chocolate eggs.*

Above *The Simnel cake is an essential part of any Easter tea.*

midsummer party

Party planning and preparations provide an excellent diversion for the long holidays. To make this summer party more of an occasion, the most unassuming garden feature, the lawn, takes centre stage – careful mowing produces the game board for the party. This ingenuous effect requires some forward planning: leave the lawn unmown for a week or two, depending on the growing conditions. Then, after marking out the proposed layout with ropes or canes, mow away sections of the lawn leaving areas of contrasting long grass which define the games. A little imagination can produce more than enough activities for an afternoon of fun.

Right *All sorts of races, like the egg and spoon race, are wonderfully exciting and use up masses of energy.*

Far right *The garden provides the ideal setting for the boisterous fun of excited party revellers.*

Below *As well as the mown lanes for the races, an array of mown paths meander through another part of the garden, criss-crossing each other and making an unpredictable selection of routes. This is an ideal area for impromptu chasing games and letting off steam.*

Right *Boule is an absorbing, almost compulsive game, which can be enjoyed by all ages, as they compete on an equal footing. It is usually played on gravel or sand, but here a court is mown into the lawn, its boundary emphasized with bright sunflower heads laid on the grass. Defining the area of the game in this way is not only appealing, it also prevents play from straying into other more boisterous activities.*

Below *All sorts of races can be run in this set of mown parallel lanes. Novelty races, such as egg and spoon or crawling backwards races, are fun and a great leveller allowing all ages to compete together. Children can devise their own programme of races and events. To help things run smoothly, have all the props needed ready at the starting line.*

Above and top *The relaxed informality of a picnic tea is suited to this kind of party. A few simple touches, such as decorative place markers and table decorations, make it feel special.*

Above and right *An unremarkable birdbath, given a touch of glamour with florist's beads and silver paint, provides the very remarkable centrepiece for the grassy game board. Filled with bubble mixture and floating flowers, it is irresistible. Set challenges to prolong the amusement – get the children to try blowing the largest bubble, catching the most bubbles, or perhaps the longest stream of bubbles in one single breath.*

Left *A shady place to eat and cool off is important after an afternoon of energetic fun. The shade canopy makes an ideal shelter, creating an intimate space in which to eat and rest.*

Below left *The luscious colours of berries in a sumptuous ice bowl makes a perfect centrepiece. Children can make the ice bowl the day before the party, picking snippets of herbs and edible flowers and arranging them in an ice bowl mould. Alternatively, use one bowl set inside another, in which you have already frozen a small amount of water to form the base. When packed with flowers, fill the mould with water and freeze overnight. To release the ice bowl from the mould simply dip it into some lukewarm water and gently work it loose.*

Below *A fragrant bunch of herbs and flowers tied with a ribbon mark the place of each guest, their name written on the shiny side of a rose leaf.*

▶ see **Shade Canopy**, page 154

halloween

In the twilight of All Hallow's Eve, the glow of grotesquely carved pumpkins, the silhouette of a hook-nosed witch and the flickering flames of huge torches create a bewitching scene to greet party guests.

This small courtyard was dressed to provide a suitably ghostly atmosphere when guests arrived for a children's Halloween party. The area also played host to a number of party games. As darkness falls, the eerie glow of pumpkin lanterns can be seen through the window adding to the feeling of mystery and magic. All the usual elements of Halloween are here, but none of the ghastly gore. Carving pumpkins, cutting out bats and reorganizing the garden takes some time, but children will enjoy making the props almost as much as they enjoy the party.

Burning candles and fires are a safety hazard. Take care that children are never left unsupervised around lit candles and fires and that all candles are securely placed and not left unattended.

Above and above right *Grouping pumpkins together gives them more impact. Lanterns burn alongside some rather more curious ones which have sprouted hair. Carving the face into the surface of the pumpkin means they can be planted with grasses. Here the ornamental grasses* Uncinia rubra *and* Ophiopogon planiscapus 'Nigrescens' *have been used. Safely out of children's reach, huge flares have a gothic feel.*

Right *Halloween celebrations are one of the best opportunities for dressing up, even for grown ups.*

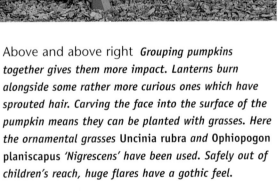

Above **The traditional game of apple bobbing is great fun, but messy and best played outside.**

Left **A host of shining bats cut from thick black polythene adorns windows, walls, plants, trellis and trees.**

Above *The window is dressed with carved pumpkin lanterns, black polythene bats, twisted twigs, silvery stars and black fabric to make a sinister backdrop.*

Above right *The leaping flames and sparks of this wrought-iron brazier, set at a safe distance, adds real drama to the scene.*

Right *These glowing lanterns are quick and simple to make. Draw a design on coloured tissue paper and cut out unwanted areas to create the design. Wrap the pieces of tissue paper around the outsides of empty jam jars, securing them with sticky tape, and add a night light.*

Above *This striking silhouette of a hook-nosed witch and her bubbling cauldron is cut from thick black polythene (black pond liner is excellent for this). Set against the light-coloured background, lit by lanterns, the scene becomes more eerie at twilight. This striking decoration can easily be rolled up and brought out again for next year's celebrations.*

Right *Children unable to take part in carving pumpkins can still contribute by designing their grotesque faces in marker pen on the skin for an adult to cut out.*

christmas

At this time of year when all else is joyful and sparkling, the garden is often forgotten. Bringing some of the colour and glamour of Christmas into the garden can provide a wonderful diversion for excited children. It is pleasant to look out on a festive scene or provide a special welcome for Christmas visitors.

The front door is an obvious place to start with the decorations, and then perhaps choose to decorate the areas most viewed from the house. If the children have a place of their own in the garden, then this can be prepared for the festive season too. Many ready-made Christmas decorations can be used outside, but it is much more rewarding for children to create their own.

the relaxing retreat

A once dilapidated summerhouse forms the focus of this garden retreat for older children. As children grow older, their needs change. There is still the need to provide for physical games like football and tennis, but more time is spent talking with friends and in quieter, less active pursuits. The garden offers a wonderful opportunity to provide a haven, a space to call their own and to share with friends. The ambience here is care-free, it is an escape, not childish but for children. The children are fortunate to have a large lawn for sporting pursuits, so this area has been designed to provide a place to relax. Within the garden there are spaces to eat, sit, laze and swing, and a separate more intimate area of deck. The summerhouse provides shelter and storage.

Evergreen grasses form the mainstay of the planting, which softens the structure of the garden. The colours chosen here are strong blues and yellows. The consistent use of these colours unites the different elements, giving the space an identity of its own and distinguishing it from the rest of the surrounding garden.

Above *A series of sturdy posts and kite fabric canopies provides a visual link between the summerhouse and the area outside, uniting the two. The four posts are simply held in position with ready-mix concrete, and form the supports for the large swinging benches either side. Using two colours of wood stain on each post creates an interesting visual effect.*

Right *Animated light and colour are projected around the garden by this hanging sheet of gleaming compact discs. Simply wired together and suspended by clothes pegs, compact discs make a novel and inexpensive decorative touch.*

148 real children's gardens

Left *Slightly apart from the rest of the retreat, a yellow deck provides an intimate space. Overhung by a natural canopy, the deck is surrounded by a swathe of evergreen grasses and bright yellow flowers. Decking is a naturally warm and welcoming surface – just add a few cushions.*

Below left *Swinging is wonderfully relaxing. This 2m (6ft) swinging bench is big enough to share with friends. It is made from a large plank of timber suspended by rope from large hooks on the posts on either side. The rope passes through holes in the corners of the seat and is knotted beneath. The canopy overhead lends the space a feeling of intimacy and protection.*

Below *Ceramic glazed jars, planted with a shimmering* **Carex** *'Frosted Curls', stand sentinel on either side of the main canopy.*

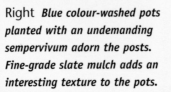

Left *Inexpensive paving stones have been transformed using masonry paint. Not only are they now more decorative, but they can be used as gaming boards as well. Set well into the grass, they can simply be passed over when mowing. Here a chessboard, noughts and crosses, and tiddly winks or a marble game have been chosen, but the possibilities are endless.*

Right *Blue colour-washed pots planted with an undemanding sempervivum adorn the posts. Fine-grade slate mulch adds an interesting texture to the pots.*

Above *Beneath a gently rustling canopy, a gaily striped hammock is the perfect place for sitting or lounging. The shorter of the two post supports is spiralled by a coil of reclaimed concrete reinforcer, painted a darker shade of blue, which plays host to the climbing plant* Thunbergia alata *(black-eyed Susan).*

Right *No special preparation is required to make these game slabs. Just mark your design on to the paving stone with pencil and fill it in with the chosen colour of paint.*

safety

Minor bumps and bruises are an acceptable part of growing up – the products of testing capabilities and learning about the world, the trophies of childhood optimism and enthusiasm. The garden is the place where children get most opportunity to test their talents and explore. The sad fact is, however, that many children suffer major injury in their own gardens.

There is a careful balance to be achieved between the desire to provide a stimulating, challenging and entertaining environment, where the basic rules about keeping safe can be learnt and practised, and the need to remove all potential hazards. To complicate matters further, the point of balance is constantly shifting; what presents a danger to a two-year-old may be an irrelevance by the age of five, while safety measures employed beyond necessity may be very restricting for older children. Every reasonable step to remove danger should be taken.

The more confident a parent can be that a child has a safe place to play, the more freedom they can allow that child. A thorough and ongoing assessment of risk is advisable, with safety measures implemented and removed as appropriate.

Perhaps the biggest risk in the garden is that from the sun. Be sure to apply sun protection lotion when the children are playing outside for long periods, even in fairly overcast weather. Another form of sun protection is a shade canopy, which is simple to make and adds an eye-catching splash of colour to the garden.

Shade Canopy • Play Surfaces • Water • Plants • Other Hazards

shade canopy

This stylish, free-standing canopy can provide a large area of essential shade wherever it is needed. It can be used to protect sandpits, paddling pools and places to eat. When placed on a sunny lawn, children are naturally drawn to play in its shelter. When the canopy is complete, add a guy rope to each post, tying it around the screw of the finial and pegging it into the ground. Ensure that the pegs are flush with the ground and the guy ropes are easily visible.

materials
4 large terracotta pots
green masonry paint
4 wooden posts, 2.25m
  (7ft 6in) long
acrylic paints or wood stains
ready-mix concrete
2 large rectangles of closely
  woven fabric
cotton
4 brass hooks
4 brass curtain rings

1 Paint the pots with green masonry paint. Paint the wooden poles and finials with acrylic paints or colourful wood stain to match. Using two colours of paint or wood stain gives an interesting effect.

2 Set a post in each pot and secure it in place using ready-mix concrete. Ensure the posts are vertical using a spirit level, and leave sufficient space at the top of the pot to allow for planting.

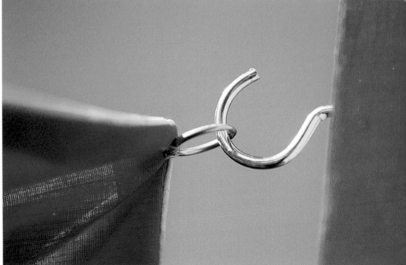

3 When the concrete is dry, add a finial to the top of each post. Sew the two pieces of fabric together, right sides in, leaving a 15cm (6in) gap in one of the seams. Turn the canopy right sides out and finish off the gap in the seam by hand.

4 Screw a brass hook 15cm (6in) from the top of each post. Sew a brass curtain ring to each end of the short sides of the canopy, 20cm (8in) in from the corners. Hook the canopy on to the posts and plant up the tops of the pots.

play surfaces

Choosing the right flooring under and around play equipment can make it safer. Surfaces which have some form of impact attenuation make injury from falls less likely. Simple grass or topsoil have some value. Other surfaces provide more protection, such as a deep layer of bark or wood chips, or specially designed rubber play matting systems, which can be laid over shock-absorbing pads. Play features should never be positioned on areas of concrete, tarmac, stone or other hard surfaces.

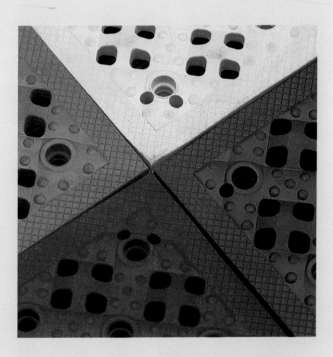

Above *This rubber play surface is bright, colourful, durable, non-slip and shock absorbent. It comes in square tiles in a range of different bright colours, and is flexible enough to be laid on sloping ground.*

Above *A beautifully designed iron grill guards the surface of this raised pond. Its ripple-like bars and lily pads actually enhance rather than detract from the pond's appearance.*

water

A young child will inevitably investigate any standing water around the garden. The alarming fact is that children can drown in just 5cm (2in) of water. Those aged between one and two years old are most at risk, with their newly acquired mobility but immature co-ordination. Some safety measures are simple; containers likely to collect a significant quantity of rain water should not be left in the garden. Take steps to secure water butts and always empty paddling pools. If there is a pond in the garden, then rigorous measures need to be taken. A rigid steel mesh can be secured over the entire surface of the pond, its integrity regularly checked. Chicken wire is just not good enough as it will sag under the weight of a child. Fencing the pond off is a solution often used. However, bear in mind that some fencing is easily climbed and gates need to be locked at all times and never inadvertently left open.

plants

It can seem that some plants are deliberately beguiling: the shining red berries of solanum (deadly nightshade) look as good as any sweet, the seedpods of laburnum could just as easily be miniature peas. In reality, however, both are extremely toxic. Other poisonous plants are not so appealing and, therefore, are less likely to present a hazard. Fortunately, instances of poisoning by plants are rare.

Plants also pose other risks: some produce an irritant or allergic reaction after contact with the plant or its sap (such as euphorbias), others present a physical danger such as sharp thorns, spines or pointed leaves.

Teach young children never to eat anything in the garden unless they have been told it is safe. Then, assess the likely risks in your garden, moving or removing plants. Exhaustive lists of poisonous and irritant plants are readily available, but space does not allow inclusion of such a list here.

Above and top **Ricinus communis (castor oil plant, top) is a strong irritant, while, once broken, the brittle stems of Euphorbia myrsinites pump out an irritant milky sap.**

other hazards

Above **The steep stairs of this terrace are safely guarded by these stylish gates.**

Children are tirelessly inquisitive – they want to experience and experiment with all they find around them. This means that a few basic safety rules need to be applied to the garden. Never leave tools or electrical equipment within reach. Lock all pesticides, fungicides and other chemicals securely away, or better still do not use them. Be aware of developmental changes in your children which give rise to new dangers, for example, as soon as a baby is mobile, steps need to be guarded. Look out for temporary hazards: the ends of the canes used for staking border plants could cause injury to running children. Using decorative cane tops makes this less likely. One final hazard is relevant when your child is outside – the sun. Provide sun creams, sun hats and, wherever possible, shade.

index

acknowledgments

Thanks to the following for the supply of materials:
Steel walkway – Goodman Steel (0118) 9561212
Glass, shell and coloured gravels – Specialist Aggregates (01785) 665554
Carnivorous plants – South West Carnivorous Plants (01884) 841549
Climbing holds – Enterprise (UK) Ltd (01282) 444800
Rubber play matting – Matta Products (01932) 788699
Rope – Footrope Knots (01473) 690090
Design of knotting for Rope Spider's Web – Des Pawson of Footrope Knots
Crocodile bench – Lusty Garden Furniture (01547) 560225
Pedro Bird Houses (p118) – Paul Hervey Decorative Products (01590) 645629
Wicker ewe and lamb sculptures (p118) at Nyewood House, Hampshire
Wooden fish sculptures (p119) at David and Marie Chase's Garden, Hampshire
Pond cover (p156) designed by Robin Templar-Williams
Decking garden (p157) designed by Sarah Layton

Author's acknowledgments
This book is the product of a very personal passion but it could not have been completed without the hard work, help and encouragement of others, to whom I owe a great debt of gratitude.

My thanks:

To my children, Harriet, Nancy and Joshua, the inspiration for this book, for their exuberance, honesty, patience and hard work throughout the project; I really could not have done it without them.

To the Hicks, Maitland and James families for allowing me to create the Real Children's Gardens in their gardens, giving me the freedom to create the unusual, for their unfailing enthusiasm, much appreciated practical help and great friendship, thank you.

To my parents, Ruth and Geoffrey Smee, for their support, encouragement, tireless practical assistance (from concrete mixing to cake baking) and their astounding and unfailing willingness to help in perpetuum.

To Clive Nichols for encouraging me to attempt this project, his enthusiasm, constant good humour and, of course, sensational photography.

To Joanna Smith for her faith in the project, her calm advice and great care over the design and editing of the book.

To Janet James for her patience and cheerfully rising to the challenge of tight deadlines in typing the manuscript.

To Steve Daley and Craig Hunt, whose generous favours saved the day.

To Hazel, Robert, Molly, Florence, Steven, Daniel, Connie, Ollie, Andy, Shana, Jasmine, William, George, Lucy, Jessica, Hannah and Anna-Nyun Forbang (pages 8, 64 and 159), who all appear in the book.

Finally to David, as always, for everything.

credits

Executive Editor Emily Van Eesteren
Executive Art Editor Tokiko Morishima
Production Controller Louise Hall
Editor and Designer Joanna Smith
All projects created and styled by Clare Matthews